Down on the Ice

by Rupert Alchin
from an interview with Rose Evans

Learning Media

Contents

1. The Letter 3

2. Training in the Mountains 10

3. On the Ice 12

4. Life at an Antarctic Station 16

5. Three Weeks at Scott's Hut 19

6. Wildlife 25

7. Coming Home 31

1. The Letter

The letter came one day early in the spring, just as the weather was getting warmer. The letter told me that I would be spending *my* summer in Antarctica. My friends at home would be playing volleyball at the beach – I would be walking about in the ice and snow.

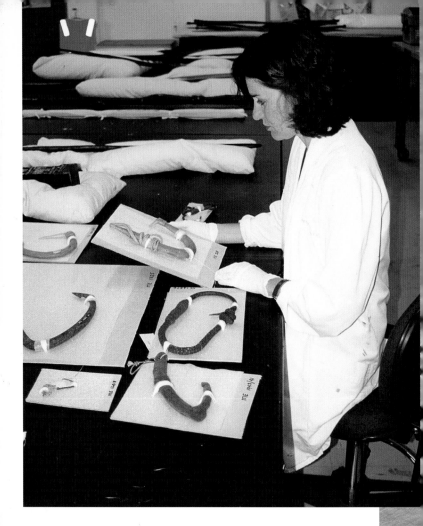

I work in a museum. Part of my job that summer was to work at the hut built in Antarctica in 1911 by a British explorer called Robert Scott.

Scott and his men traveled to Antarctica on a sailing ship called the Terra Nova.

I was going to spend three weeks studying the hut and everything left there by Scott and his men.

This hut was Scott's base for his journey to the South Pole. He dreamed of being the first explorer to get there. He and his men traveled over 2,000 miles inland on foot. After terrible hardships, they finally reached the South Pole.

Inside Scott's Hut

But they were *not* the first – some explorers from Norway had got there a month before them. Scott and his men were very disappointed – and they still had to make the journey back!

Scott and his men never made it back to their hut on the coast. On the way home, they were hit by many blizzards. The five men were weak and hungry, and they had frostbite. With only 18 miles to go, a howling storm set in. The men were trapped in their tent for over a week.

Pulling the supplies in soft snow was very hard work.

Scott and his men at the South Pole

The temperature was down to minus 86°F! One by one, the men died of cold and hunger.

> we shall stick it out
> to the end but we
> are getting weaker of
> course and the end
> cannot be far
> It seems a pity but
> I do not think I can
> write more —
> R Scott

In his diary, Scott wrote:
"We shall stick it out to the end, but we are getting weaker, of course, and the end cannot be far. It seems a pity, but I do not think I can write more."

2. Training in the Mountains

Antarctica is a very dangerous place. So, before we went there, a group of us had to spend a week at a camp in the mountains.

We had lots of talks about the dangers of life in Antarctica. We had to learn how to stop ourselves if we started to slide on the ice. When you slide on ice or snow, you speed up very quickly. If you can't stop right away, you can be badly hurt. You have to roll over and dig your ice pick into the snow. This is called "self-arresting."

After the mountain training, we traveled to Antarctica. We had another week of training there. I thought it was cold in the mountains, but it was far worse in Antarctica.

3. On the Ice

This training was really hard! We had to make caves in the snow – then we had to spend the night in one! I lay there all night on the hard ground, with my face nearly touching the snow.

It was cold, but my sleeping bag was really warm. I slept very well!

Next morning, I crawled out of my snow cave feeling quite good. Then it was straight into some "crevasse training."

Crevasses are big cracks in the ice. They can be thirty feet wide and hundreds of feet deep. Often they're covered with a thin lid of snow and ice, so you can't see them. But if you walk out onto the thin ice it can break, and then down you go. We had to be roped together for safety.

The leader goes ahead, poking the snow with an ice pick to check for crevasses. It's a bit like following a giant hen as it pecks at the ice.

Sometimes, one of the team falls into a crevasse. If that happens, everyone else has to "self-arrest" so that they don't slide over the edge too. The person who fell climbs back up the rope to safety.

4. Life at an Antarctic Station

We didn't spend all our time training. When we first arrived, we stayed at Scott Base. That's New Zealand's Antarctic station.

It wasn't far to McMurdo, the American base. I liked going there because it was so different from Scott Base.

To me, Scott Base was like a space station. There were lots of huts joined up by tunnels – a bit like big green fridges joined by tubes. It was colder there than at McMurdo, so everyone wore warm clothes. It looked like they were wearing big, puffy spacesuits.

McMurdo was really different. The main buildings looked like big factories. There was a church up on the hill and lots of lodges where everyone lived. The people all looked very relaxed. It was just like being in a small American town.

5. Three Weeks at Scott's Hut

After all the training, it was finally time to start my real work – three weeks out at Scott's Hut. My co-worker and I were going to be alone out in the wilderness.

I would really miss life at the bases – no more lovely hot showers. I would also miss the midsummer swim at Scott Base. The water there would be just above freezing temperature!

We went to Scott's Hut by helicopter and moved into a little hut called a wanigan.

Every morning, it took us about two hours to make breakfast and melt enough water for our day's work. It's so cold down there, and you feel really tired all the time. Even very simple jobs seem to take forever.

After breakfast, we'd push open the door and stumble out into the wind. Then it was a ten-minute walk over the ice and snow to Scott's Hut.

It was so good to get inside the hut, away from the cold wind.

Going into the hut was like stepping back in time. It was quite spooky, like diving down to the *Titanic*.

Everything was just like Scott's men had left it. The shelves were filled with rusty old cans of food and other supplies. There were old sweaters and ski boots lying around.

The laboratory and darkroom looked the same as they had when Scott's team used them. Maybe I could have developed my photos there too!

CAPT. SCOTT'S ANTARCTIC
EXPEDITION 1910
"HOMELIGHT"
LAMP OIL

6. Wildlife

When I wasn't working, I spent a lot of time watching the animals. There were always lots of seals on shore. They looked very cute and friendly, but when they yawned, you could see their big sharp teeth.

The most wonderful creatures were the killer whales. Sometimes they would swim up and down the beach, watching the seals and penguins.

That reminded me of something I'd read in Scott's diary. The men were unloading supplies onto the ice. Scott looked up and saw a group of whales swim up near the shore and then dive under.

A few seconds later, there was a cracking sound. The ice the men were standing on broke up into big chunks. The whales had pushed it from below. The men had to race for their lives to get to solid ground.

Soon the whales' heads bobbed above the water. They were checking to see if they'd knocked anyone into the sea!

Lots of the animals weren't frightening – just annoying. The penguins were always curious, pecking at everything. I don't think I've ever met a nosier bunch of birds.

The skua birds
spent all day
squawking at each
other and fighting over food. They are
very clever birds. They spent a lot of
time working out how to get into our
food supplies.

By the end of my time in Antarctica, I was starting to look like one of the animals myself.

Down on the ice, your face can get very tanned – except for white patches around your eyes where your sunglasses have been. When we were picked up from the hut at the end of the three weeks, I looked like an 800-year-old raccoon!

7. Coming Home

Getting back home was wonderful. It was still summer. The warm days and all the smells were wonderful. I could sleep in real sheets and take a bath. And I didn't have to melt gallons of water every day!

SCOTT AA BASE
CANTERBURY

KILOMETERS TO

SOUTH POLE 1353	CHRISTCHURCH 3832
WELLINGTON 4080	CANBERRA 4807
SANTIAGO 7079	BUENOS AIRES 7160
CAPE TOWN 7408	TOKYO 12760
WASHINGTON 14828	PARIS 16708
MOSCOW 16899	BRUSSELS 16930
LONDON 17039	OSLO 17839

I soon got used to being home. I felt like my time on the ice was far in the past. But in some ways I had changed. Being alone down on the ice was special.

Sometimes in the summer, when I'm at the beach with my friends, I look toward the south. I remember my adventure in that strange, distant land.